Half Naked Closings

*Real World Lessons
About Real Estate Transactions*

By Hugh Fitzpatrick III, ESQ

Table of Contents

Introduction 1

The Elderly Half-Naked Woman 5

The 'Destroyed' Dining Room Table 15

The Inebriated Seller 25

The Emotional FSBO 37

The European Closings 47

Conclusion 55

Introduction

For more than half of my adult life, I have been helping people buy, sell or finance their homes in New England. Having participated in thousands of closings, I have seen many things, things that you would never think would happened in a real estate transaction. In the utopian world of law school, I learned how real estate worked and how to represent the interests of sellers, buyers and mortgage companies. Unfortunately, that legal education did not prepare me to handle real world issues.

That was something I learned on my own through years of experience and thousands of transactions.

As you probably know, real world lessons are not always easy, which is why I want to share some of my experiences to help those involved in this process. These stories are handpicked from an array of fascinating tales, tales that, at times, sound simply unbelievable, but believe me, everything that I'm writing actually happened. As I recall these experiences, I reflect on the people involved, wondering how they every made it through the deal.

Buying or selling real estate can be an extremely emotional situation. There tends to be a lot riding on the transaction which can trigger a negative emotional experience when things don't go as planned. In many cases, I find myself playing more the role of therapist than counsel as I reassure yet another client on the edge that we will make it through this. Though simple in theory but difficult to do, my advice to clients who are becoming overly distraught is to try to not be emotionally involved. Emotions cloud your judgement and get in the way of making objective and, let's face it, smart decisions. However, this is often challenging and I understand their concerns, having gone through this process in my life as well. My hope in writing about my closing tales is that the reader can identify and learn from my experiences since many of us have been involved in our own 'nightmare closings.'

Enjoy.

Hugh Fitzpatrick III, ESQ

The Elderly Half-Naked Woman

Yes, I was trying to lure you in with the title, but this tale is actually based upon a real life experience. In 2004, our company received a request from a reverse mortgage company to conduct a closing on their behalf. In Massachusetts where I practice, an attorney can be involved in many different stages of a real estate transaction and potentially represent the interests of parties ranging from sellers and buyers to lenders. On this particular deal, my client was the lender, the reverse mortgage company who asked me to close the loan and provide, amongst other things, an opinion of title along with escrow and title insurance. Now most folks don't really know what an attorney does on real estate deal. They know that they should have one, but often don't know why. It's because of this that I make sure to explain the process to my clients as well as those on the other side of the transaction, just to make sure everyone is on the same page.

I had completed all of the tasks that my client had asked of me and was ready to close the loan. I had been in touch with the borrower throughout the process, explaining how my company had been hired by her lender, the reverse mortgage company, to close the loan on its behalf. I also explained that I would be contacting her soon to sign the documents necessary to close the loan.

The time arrived for closing and I called the borrower to ask when and where she'd like to conduct the closing. She was silent for some time, so I asked her again. She stated that she always thought closings were conducted at the attorney's office and was surprised that she could choose the location. I explained to her that we could certainly do that, but since my company recognizes, that as a service business, it was important to be accommodating to our customers, which is why we offer a choice of closing locations. There was another long pause. As I readied myself to ask the question for a third time she said, almost wistfully, that it would be nice to close in her home.

Now that we had the time and location established, I prepared the loan package that she would need to sign. Once the packet of documents was ready, I made my way to the borrower's home in Lowell, Massachusetts, the next town over from our office location. Having attended college in Lowell, I knew exactly where I was going and, during the short, ten-minute trip, I recalled some of the wild nights from those days and silently wondered if I might have partied at her house. Curiosity got the better of me, so I pulled over and quickly reviewed the title report to see how long she'd owned the house. Thankfully, she had owned the property for over twenty years, eliminating the possibility of what may have been some awkward feelings on my part, or so I thought.

I pulled into her driveway and proceeded to the side door because it appeared to be the entrance used most often. I rang the bell and knocked, just in case the bell didn't work – no answer. I waited a minute or two and tried again. Still no answer. Starting to feel a bit annoyed, I tried one more time.

A moment later, an elderly lady answered the door. She was completely naked from the waist up. Without pause, and certainly without the discomfort I was clearly feeling at this unusual encounter, she says "hello, let me just put my shirt on, but please come in." Finding myself at a total loss for words and unable to think of any other appropriate plan of action, I followed instructions as if nothing out of the ordinary had just happened.

I sat at her kitchen table and waited for her to reappear. She returned, thankfully now fully clothed, and said that she was ready to sign the paperwork. Now it was my turn to pause.

As the seconds turned into a minute, I was finally able to ask "are you sure you wanted to sign the papers?" She replied, "yes, why wouldn't I?" Recalling my legal training on the subject of competency, I thought to myself, is she crazy or was she hitting on me? Despite my discomfort with the possibility of it being the latter, professionally, I knew I needed to verify that this individual was competent and signing the closing documents freely and voluntarily. So I tried to remain objective as I carefully asked a few questions to establish her level of competency. Satisfied that she did indeed know what she was doing, I decided to start the closing.

During the actual signing of the paperwork, I listened closely and answered her questions about the subject matter. Despite our unusual introduction, I was impressed with her questions. She asked very intelligent questions about her title and the protections of homestead in our state and, once all the documents were complete, she politely escorted me to the door and wished me a good day.

Once in my car, I let out a long breath and said to myself "even if the Good Lord allows me to practice for another fifty years, I am sure I will never see anything like that again."

Thankfully, so far I have not. Remembering this situation, I remind myself that although there are certain commonalities to each deal, each is unique in their own way, some more than others! Preparing yourself to handle these 'interesting' transactions will keep your organization sharp and will hold you in good stead with your clients. Have an open mind when handling each and every deal and, above all, be prepared for the unexpected.

The 'Destroyed' Dining Room Table

Sometime in September 2007, I received a phone message from one of our lender clients. As I listened to my voicemail, I began to get a knot in my stomach. My firm had represented one of the nation's top five lenders for over fifteen years. The relationship was pretty hands-off. Other than my twice annual trips to its corporate headquarters, I hardly ever spoke to the 'big boss,' so when I heard his voice on the other end of the phone I knew the news couldn't be good.

His message didn't contain anything substantive, just a request to call him back when I had a moment. He also left his cell phone so I knew he expected an immediate response. Before I made the call, I asked my team if there were any issues to report with our client. No one was aware of any. With no real information, I took a depth breath and dialed. He answered immediately.

"Hi Hugh, how are you?"

That was the extent of our small talk. Getting right to the heart of the matter, he tells me that he had been notified that one of our attorneys had 'destroyed' a dining room table at a closing that took place the other day. I asked if he had details on what had taken place as this was certainly an unusual situation. He said he would forward the email he'd received and requested that I personally take care of it. "Of course," was my response and with that, our conversation was done.

In less than a minute, my inbox had a new message. I opened it, read through the chain, and could quickly see that the table had been damaged when one of our attorneys set his briefcase on it. The borrower was enraged and demanding some kind of recompense. As I mulled over how to best handle this situation, I called the attorney to get his side of the story. I got him on the phone immediately and ask him about this closing.

"Do you remember any issues on this closing?"

"No, why what's up?"

I told him about the damaged table and how the borrower was extremely upset. He was honestly surprised as the borrower had never mentioned the table, that everything had gone smoothly. He was completely unaware of any damage. So clearly, the damage had been accidental, not that I ever thought anyone on my team would deliberately destroy personal property, but it was certainly a relief to hear.

At that point, I knew I needed to call the borrower. Before I called, I reread the email mail chain, paying particularly attention to the borrower's tone. He was clearly very angry, he wanted someone's neck for this one. Remembering my old firm where we routinely handled civil litigation cases, I recalled the advice that my old boss had shared about handling emotionally charged situations. He fondly referred to the process as 'defusing bombs.' With his words running through my head, I dialed the borrower's number.

As soon as I told him who I was he immediately started to yell, letting loose a string of curses that would surely have made a sailor blush. I listened to him, not saying a word. When he was done, I calmly asked "how can we make this right?" He hesitated for a moment. I'm sure he was expecting an unpleasant exchange and was taken by surprise by my calm demeanor. He finally responded by requesting that I personally come see the damage.

"Ok, when would be a good time?"

I was hoping that he wasn't going to take me up on the offer but he did.

"Can you come tomorrow?" he asked.

I had a full schedule the next day, but this situation needed my attention. I am extremely grateful for the work that the lender had provided us over the years and this was an opportunity to show them how much I valued that relationship. With that in mind, I cancelled all of my appointments and travelled two hours to see the damaged table for myself.

When I arrived at the borrower's home, he actually looked surprised to see me. He welcomed me in and offered me a cup of coffee, which I accepted. As I looked around the house, I saw some family pictures on the wall and began to ask him about this family. I could tell that he was proud of his kids and their accomplishments. Talk soon turned to the table and its history.

The table had been made by his grandfather and was a treasured family possession. I began to understand why this was such an emotional issue for him and asked whether it could be fixed. Fortunately, it could. He had already spoken to a repair shop and had an estimate to repair the damage. It was not cheap, and I'm not ashamed to say I did a double take when I was presented with the bill, but I knew what needed to be done. I opened my bag, took out the company checkbook and paid him. I cannot effectively communicate the look on his face but needless to say, he was surprised. I presented the check, shook his hand and embarked on my two-hour journey back to the office.

A few days later, the 'big boss' called me again. When I answered his call, he said just two things:

"Thank you for taking care of this situation and thank you for reconfirming my decision to do business with your firm."

That check was one of the best investments I've ever made.

When an attorney has a real estate practice, they must acknowledge that the single most important component of their business is the relationships they hold with other providers in the space. Don't look at each deal as a single transaction, look at each one as another brick in the building of a solid business relationship. Transaction-based dealings won't get you far in an industry based on trust in an individual's skill and integrity. Plan to build long lasting relationships with like-minded providers to build a network dedicated to helping people realize the dream of homeownership.

The Inebriated Seller

I have often felt that many consumers don't fully know what an attorney does in a real estate transaction. Typically, our work is overshadowed by the real estate agents and loan professionals. The agents help facilitate and hold real estate transactions together while the loan professionals provide the financing to make it all happen. Attorneys tend to have limited visibility, working behind the scenes on the legal components of the transaction.

On this particular occasion, I had an old client contact me indicating that he was interested in relocating to a different part of Massachusetts. After a brief conversation, I suggested that he engage the services of a buyer agent familiar with the area in which he wanted to purchase a new home and offered my assistance in finding one. Collectively, we had a few phone interviews with some agents trying to determine the best fit for the client and, having decided on one, my client started his search for a new home.

After visiting a few properties, my client found one he liked and inquired about submitting an offer. I encouraged him to work with the agent to settle on an offer price, but asked that I be sent the offer form so I could review it. At this point, the agent became defensive.

"Why do you need to review the form? I've been doing this for over twenty years, I've got this."

Calmly, I explained that an offer form can be considered an actual contract for sale and I wanted to verify that the form she was submitting did not obligate my client to buy the property. Puzzled and clearly frustrated, she agreed to send the form to me even though she 'didn't have any idea' what I was talking about. This was a 'standard' form that she'd been using for years without problem.

Unfortunately, many people are not aware of the legal complexities of what may appear to be a 'standard' real estate transaction, even those who conduct them every day as part of their job. Even in a so called 'standard transaction,' it can get a little muddled as to who is representing who. For instance, if the buyer didn't come direct to you as is the case in a referral, an attorney must fully examine their role in the transaction to know who the client is.

Simply, in a residential real estate transaction, the client is either the buyer, seller or mortgage company. It is never the agent. I work with many wonderful and professional agents each and every day, but I cannot let my actions be dictated by the risk of a deal falling through or the potential loss of future referrals from a disgruntled agent. My obligation as an attorney is always to the individual who retained me, be it the buyer, seller or mortgage company. In this case, I needed to represent the best interests of my client, the buyer, and that meant reviewing this 'standard' offer form, even if it resulted in some tension between me and the agent.

After I reviewed the form, the agent submitted an offer that the seller accepted. As part of the transaction, our client attended a home inspection which showed the property was in good stead, so we went forward to execute a purchase and sale agreement. As I was gathering additional details about the transaction, I discovered that the sellers were going through a bitter divorce. Divorce can add some complexities to a deal as emotions are already high, especially if the split is not amicable. I could already see that this was going to be one of those emotionally charged events. As is customary, I called the seller and asked if he was represented by counsel.

"I'm paying enough to my divorce attorney. I will be representing myself for this sale."

Oh boy, I thought. This was going to be a rough ride. If given the choice, I would always prefer to work with another attorney rather than a non-attorney for two reasons:

One could say that I have an unfair advantage based upon my legal training.

Real estate transaction are contracts and the negotiations should always be handled by a trained legal professional.

I know many people choose to forego legal representation in a real estate deal, but I always strongly recommend using an attorney to handle the legal components of a transaction. Many think that using a real estate agent is enough to protect their interests, but that's not case. Only an attorney is equipped to recognize and address the legal implications of a transaction and truly protect one's best interests.

During the negotiation of this particular contract, I could tell that the seller was angry, most likely due to his domestic situation. Despite the lack of appropriate counsel on the seller's side, we were able to successfully negotiated the terms of a purchase and sale and move toward a closing.

Closing day finally arrived and I began reviewing the paperwork prior to the meeting. As with most law firms in Massachusetts, while the lawyer is personally involved in many aspects of the transaction, a paralegal manages much of the other work so I wanted to be sure that everything was in order and prepared to our firm's standards. As I reviewed the paperwork, I recalled how difficult the seller had been at the beginning of this deal and hoped that he would be more reasonable at the closing itself. Unfortunately, that was not to be the case.

From my desk, I could hear some folks entering the office. Shortly after they entered, the quiet murmur of normal conversation escalated to loud screaming. I quickly made my way to the waiting room to see what was happening. As I moved closer, I recognized the angry voice as that of the seller.

I moved forward quickly into the waiting area, greeted everyone and asked what was the cause of all of the commotion. The seller ignored me and continued his rant. I stood in front of him and asked very calmly if he would he like to come to my office and talk about what had him so upset. He surprised me by immediately calming and then accepting my invitation to talk.

"So what's going on?" I asked.

As I awaited his response, I couldn't help but notice the overwhelming smell of alcohol in my office. After listening to his incoherent response, I realized that this guy was drunk, really drunk. Recognizing that his competency for signing documentation was now compromised, I knew I could not proceed with the closing. I gathered all the parties and explained that we could not conduct the closing that day. We found another time that worked for all involved and I executed an extension of the purchase and sale agreement to protect the interests of my buyer.

So while common sense might dictate this to most, I'll state it clearly here – do not show up to a real estate closing drunk. And, as an attorney, certainly don't proceed with the transaction if one of the parties is clearly compromised.

I have often suggested that an experienced real estate attorney is like a home plate umpire guiding the transaction, making sure that the players know their position and that everyone is playing by the rules. Like the umpire, a good attorney needs to keep his eye on the game and be ready to make the calls that ensure a fair and well-played game.

The Emotional FSBO

A while back, my brother in-law and I were having a conversation at a family birthday party. He wanted to get my opinion about selling his house and moving to another town. Both of us share a common trait in that we like to carefully weigh the benefits and risk of each decision that we make, especially a housing decision. During the conversation, I started with my typically questions of why do you want to move, to what town, what's your pricing, etc. Knowing that he had already made up his mind about doing it, I shared the same advice that I do with all of my real estate clients:

"Buying and selling a home is an extremely emotional experience. You must prepare your family for the challenges that you will face."

At the time, I don't think he fully comprehended the gravity of what I was saying or maybe he thought I was being overly dramatic. However, a few days later, we spoke once again and he declared that everyone was now prepared. In an interesting exercise, we graphed out all of the possible outcomes. One of the first decisions that we weighed was whether to sell his house using a real estate agent or on his own. I could tell that he was leaning towards not using an agent so as to save on the commission fee. I cautioned him against going it alone, advising him that agents have more experience in getting a true value for the home and moreover, reminded him that selling a home is emotionally demanding and that it's better to have someone who is an impartial party who can handle the deal without being influenced by emotion. I suggested that he meet with some agents and negotiate the fee for sale.

Many people don't realize that you can negotiate the commission paid on a sale. Taking my advice, my brother in-law and engaged the services of a reputable agent to not only sell his current home, but also assist in the purchase of the new one, all at a commission rate with which he was comfortable.

In a bit of a surprise, the agent that was representing him came across a property that was for sale by owner (FSBO). Since it was not listed with a broker, the property was getting limited exposure and not many people knew that the property was up for sale. In my experience, agents are quite good at getting the word out that your house is for sale which is one of the many benefits of using one. A good agent will typically list your house on many online platforms, conduct open house events and put the traditional, highly visible 'For Sale' sign in front of your house. It soon became clear that the FSBO seller had made little effort to market the property.

Another benefit of hiring an experienced agent to sell your home is the agent's understanding of current market value. To determine the price of your home, an agent will look at recent sales of similar properties in the area. These are commonly referred to as comps (comparisons) and help the agent arrive at a selling price that will not only get you the best value for your home, but also ensure that it sells quickly.

My brother in-law and his family toured the FSBO property with their agent and decided that they wanted to make an offer. Since clearly very little had been done to properly sell the property, I advised that they not only have their agent take a look at comps in the area, but also employ a real estate appraiser to ensure that they didn't offer too much for the property. As it turns out, the appraiser concluded that the list price for the FSBO was actually quite low in comparison to recent comparable sales. With this knowledge in hand, my brother in-law quickly made an offer for the full selling price which was accepted by the sellers. He and my sister were quite pleased with themselves and were looking forward to moving into their new home that they were purchasing for a relative bargain.

Unfortunately, many things can go wrong between the acceptance of an offer and the transfer of title and this sale was one of those situations. Shortly after signing the purchase and sale agreement, the sellers realized that they had agreed to sell their property for less than market value. Realizing their mistake, the sellers became extremely difficult to deal with, making every attempt to make the transaction as difficult as possible. Every interaction was part of an uncooperative pattern of behavior, as they did all they could to frustrate my brother in-law into abandoning the transaction. Knowing what a sweet deal they were getting, I advised him to remain calm and to keep pushing forward, knowing that we would eventually get the deal done.

Oddly enough, the sellers did not attend the closing, likely annoyed that their tactics didn't work, and the transfer of title was finally completed.

The lesson here, it's typically a worthwhile investment to engage an experienced agent whether you're buying or selling a property. A good agent will establish a fair price for a property on either side of a transaction and save you from many pitfalls along the way, including buyer's or seller's remorse.

Additionally, when you engage in an attorney to help you along this way, I would suggest that you shop around, call a few to get an understanding of their real estate practice. Real estate counsel must be readily accessible to you to not only provide solid, legal advice, but also provide a levelheaded point-of-view when the going gets rough and emotion clouds your judgement.

The European Closings

Representing one of the largest mortgage lenders in the country creates many opportunities for some interesting closings. In early 2003, our client called to let us know that they wanted a closing done in West Germany and expected it to be done by the end of the week. This may seem atypical to many, but our company has always operated under the mission of being customer-centric and one of our services included closing at a location of the client's choosing and as expediently as possible. That being said, I remember thinking that they couldn't actually expect us to fly to West Germany for the closing. In fact, I was reasonably sure that even if I could get there on such short notice, there must be some legal restriction that would prevent me from personally closing in West Germany. Needing more information, I called the lender.

It turns out that I would not be going to West Germany but, in fact, would attend the closing by phone. Knowing that this might entail some additional challenges, I worked directly with the lender and their counsel to gain a better understanding of the inner workings of this deal.

In Massachusetts, an attorney must "substantially participate" in a real estate closing as defined by a series of court cases. With this legal standard in mind, the lender is charged with meeting these requirements regardless of the physical location of the closing. As we conferred about the transaction, it became clear that the house being refinanced was registered land which added another level of complexity to the deal. For those who don't know, Massachusetts has two types of land registration, recorded land and registered land. When your property is registered land, title to your property is guaranteed by the Commonwealth of Massachusetts. At the time of writing, Massachusetts is the only state that has both types of land registration.

As I began my research on conducting an out of the country closing, I called my title insurance company and the chief title examiner for the Commonwealth. The chief title examiner is essential the gatekeeper for the Commonwealth for getting documents recorded. He would provide me with the necessary information on how to execute the notarization part of the closing. If the notarization was not done correctly, we would not be able to record the mortgage, which is a vital step to the closing process. I called him and briefly explained the situation. He then asked two questions:

Where was the closing taking place?

Who was the notary involved?

I knew that the closing would take place at the American Embassy, but I didn't have any information on the notary. I quickly called the lender to inquire.

My contact told me that the notary was someone inside the embassy commissioned to administer oaths and take acknowledgments. Feeling comfortable with this information, I presented this new information to the chief title examiner. He listened to this updated information, and confidently said "you should be fine." Now, I don't typically like to work with such conditional information, but time was running short, and my resources to verify his assurance were limited.

As luck would have it, my team, as well as that of the lenders', had all the necessary resources in place and the closing went off without a hitch. My first European closing was conducted without ever having set foot in the country where the closing took place.

Real estate closings are process-driven and repetitive, but not always predictable. The real estate closing business will always present many challenges, some common and other unique like those chronicled in this book. When conducting a real estate deal, make sure that you are working with an organization that is nimble, one that can move out of its own way if needed and adjust quickly to changes. The quality of your representation will show itself when the unexpected appears.

Conclusion

For most of us, buying, selling or refinancing a property is probably one of the biggest and most important decisions that one will ever make. In looking at the service providers in a real estate transaction – the listing agent, the buyer's agent, mortgage officer and attorney – I have always contended that home buyers and sellers must have an independent voice that can serve as their advocate during this often difficult and emotional process. An experienced real estate attorney should be your first call when embarking on any real estate transaction, as your attorney will always hold your best interests as their highest priority.

www.ingramcontent.com/pod-product-compliance
Lightning Source LLC
Chambersburg PA
CBHW070333190526
45169CB00005B/1871